C000216286

FOWEY
Source to sea

SUE LEWINGTON

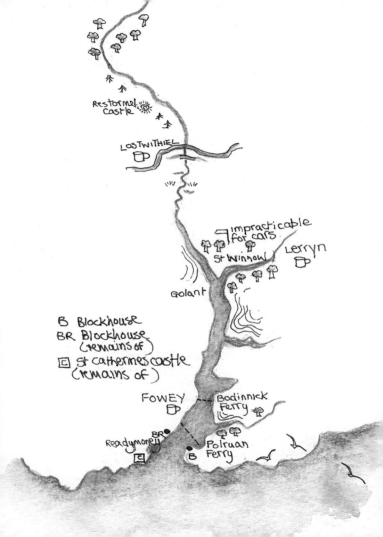

Restormel Castle

LOSTWITHIEL

impracticable for cars
St Winnow
Lerryn

Golant

B Blockhouse
BR Blockhouse (remains of)
C St Catherines castle (remains of)

FOWEY
Bodinnick Ferry

Readymoney BR
C
B Polruan Ferry

F the source hills

empty hills

hills

hills

FOWEY

- ~~~ small lanes
- ~~~ busy roads
- ''''' bracken/heath
- ~~~ marshy r wet
- ☕ coffee
- F ☕ coffee (flask)
- F ☕ forgot the flask
- ♣♣ woods

Ford r foot bridge

F ☕

busy road

small bridge
cyclists r runners LOST...

This is not a real map
I have tried to condense
a very long river on to
two small pages.
I was lost a lot of the
time r, to begin with,
rarely sure which
bridge I was at ...
The forgotten flask
was a major crisis

F ☕ ♣ Draynes bridge

♣♣ Golitha Falls

busy road

Respryn bridge

ISBN 978 185022 242 2

First published in 2013 by Truran
an imprint of Tor Mark

Tor Mark
United Downs Ind. Est.
St. Day
Redruth
TR16 5HY

www.truranbooks.co.uk

Printed & bound in Cornwall by
R. Booth Ltd
The Praze
Penryn
Cornwall
TR10 8AA

I remember most the two extremes
of the Fowey.
The tiny stream following the
snaking valleys through bare hills
on Bodmin Moor & the flat expanse
reflecting the sky between Fowey
& Polruan.
Between these two are twists & turns,
wooded valleys, white water at
Golitha, hidden miles & ancient
bridges
At Golant, as the tide falls, I'm glad
to see small stream again snaking
between banks of shining mud
before it disappears between the
blockhouses & away to the horizon.

on Bodmin Moor

The path is almost wet enough to be a
stream – Downhill the Fowey has to
be down here somewhere. . . .

A ford – too deep to cross
& flowing fast

Found it
The footbridge near the ford

Hidden by undergrowth
Tiny... but the first bridge

Walking into the moor - the river is hidden, but its sinuous track easy to spot.

Its not like the high Penwith
moors where the granite breaks
through all over.
Here are long, whale back hills,
deceptive distances, quiet & stillness.

Too wet lower down,
up here the fields are bare
& the walls broken. An open
& empty landscape

I've been walking a while & the source
of the Fowey is somewhere along the
winding valley in front. I'd have to
make my way over the high ground
on the right — too muddy walking
lower down.

A tiny farmstead the last before
↓ The bare moors. I can't see
any road leading to it . . . .

It looks a long way ~ & I didn't bring
a flask . . . . .
So . . . This is as close as I get to the
source ~ I'm making my way back
to the car . . . .

The path isn't quite
where I thought it should be,
but I hope that curve of trees
at the foot of the hill is the tiny
path back to the road.

The river glints as it winds slowly round the feet of the hills.

The main road is hidden in the landscape, overpowered by the empty hills.

All the trees down near the water
are hung with this strange long
pale lichen. It looks odd - exotic
against the bare hills.

Back to the ford..

climbing steeply back up
from the Ford...

to the isolated farm at the top.

Down the tiny road from Bolventor

Harder to follow now. The narrow road has been blocked by two cars having a bit of an argument. There's a cycle race going on & masses of runners too. Nowhere to stop safely. A lovely day though-

"And I thought a sunday would be quiet!"

Nothing seems the same as the
old (1949) book I'm following

- or the modern map . . . .

the road r the river run for
miles side by side. . .

There are modern bridges
beside old fords

At last – an old bridge

But I'm lost so I don't know
what its called . . .

This one though
is Draynes Bridge.

A strange contradiction here - a tidy
path to walk, but the river becomes
wilder - full of tumbled boulders
& tree roots .

Golittia Falls
Now the river is different.
White water & dark boulders
all energy & noise
Moss covers trees & boulders alike

I dont want to leave all this energy
to try to find the river-tamed
again by banks, bridges & busy
roads. So I drive, getting lost, &
found until somehow I find
Respryn & its ancient bridge &
the river becomes itself again.

Respryn

obviously built for horse &
foot-traffic — Beautiful
shapes & aged stone
The river is wider & shallow
here. Airy & open now &
flowing on hidden from modern
life & roads.

Restormel
I'm trying to imagine the landscape before houses & roads — A stone castle sitting on the highest point overlooking the river & its water meadows. Now the railway runs alongside & the bridge is modern & dull....

I got lost on the way to
Lostwithiel & end up driving in
over this bridge instead of the new
one - lovely.

SINGLE
TRAFFIC
BRIDGE

A bridge as lovely as Respryn.
Many centuries old . . . Dating from
maybe the 14th century. Lostwithiel
has been a coinage town, a county
town, a rich & important centre,
when these tiny lanes were not backwaters
but main highways through the
county.

And it is the place where the tide begins to make itself felt.

St Winnow

The river is wide & flat here & it
doesn't seem to be moving - just
reflecting back the sky.

one of my favourite signposts

IMPRACTICABLE FOR CARS

Quite a few of the lanes between here &
Bodinnick should have signs like this
when the hedges brush _both_ sides
of the car I start to get worried . . .

Lerryn not strictly on the Fowey
but not to be missed. The stepping
stones hidden.

Down the tiny lane to
Golant..,
And the tide is way out. The
railway bridge spans mud
without the light from the water
washing up close to the road & The
houses, the colours & tones are all
darker. But out further the mud
shines & I can see the river,
narrow again, flowing on quietly.

Fowey

I like to walk in from the Caffa Mill
car park. The ferry still looks like
a shed on a raft.

Passage street follows the river. Narrow
& shaded, past the old ferry slip.
stepping into doorways to avoid
passing cars ...

A view of the river, green
& still. A perfect place
to write notes & drink
coffee.

Every thing in here is warm & bright-
& pink - including the cake.

FOWEY TOWN BUS
STOPS HERE EVERY 15 MINS

people-watching on the quay. The Polruan ferry
comes & goes. Overlooked here — as in most
parts of the old town — by the church
& Place House.

only the ferry going back & forth
Nothing on the buoys. I'm sorry the
big old tug boats aren't there
— But the sea & the horizon
at last.

A house near here is
called Polly's leap.
I'm dizzy just looking over the wall

'Q's House

Readymoney cove at the end
of the Esplanade.
St Catherines castle, on the headland
to the right, guards the entrance
to the river & the town. This is a
sea-side cove - the river is gone.

on the ferry . . .

over to Adrian.
And its very different. Much more a
working/fishing port.

As usual — this is the but I really like
Real, working boats

Rust & colous; noise & work.

I thought I was imagining it but no, the
yellow boat up on the slip was being
winched slowly down into the water.

its January & there are roses
blooming along the way to the
Blockhouse

looking back to Pont Pill over
Polruan quay

well this is as far as the road goes —
through the blockhouse & onto the rocks.
Only now do I get an overall feel of the
river — looking up from the small views
& wondering at how that tiny, snaking,
shallow stream deep in the moor has
become this enormous contained mass
which is neither sea nor river.
It pleases me that it has grown in strength
& importance until it becomes part of
something so much bigger.
I could become quite philosophical here...

But I'm going to head back for a coffee
& another slice of the beetroot cake
with the pink icing . . .